My Life and Poetry

My Life and Poetry

BIBHAKAR DUTTA

PARTRIDGE
A Penguin Company

Copyright © 2013 by Bibhakar Dutta.

ISBN: Softcover   978-1-4828-0159-0
               Ebook   978-1-4828-0158-3

Partridge books may be ordered through booksellers or by contacting:

Partridge India
Penguin Books India Pvt.Ltd
11, Community Centre, Panchsheel Park, New Delhi 110017
India
www.partridgepublishing.com
Phone: 000.800.10062.62

Contents

A Class

A beautiful morning!
It begins with delicious foods.
Multistoried buildings showing
an extra dignity to the dignified fellows are no doubt
great.
Android, tablet, laptops performing
exciting activities are no doubt perfect.
A class! really higher class . . .
Yes, I also have these (Ha! Ha!).
Suddenly, I placed my eyes into a boy.
He has a dusty sack except having a toy.
Now, I am watching him deeply.
I got his face slippery.
He is a dweller of a slum.
Now, he want to make wet his tongue
seeking some food.
Do you know, what the expensive articles are in his bag?
He gathers your damaged glasses, your furniture, our
toilet mugs . . . .
He wants to exchange it
to get his living a little bit.
Alas! What a class!
You know this class.
I will be happiest one
If I would get him a class.
He needs a class . . .

A Dark Night

It is a dark night.
I think—
I want to write and write . . . .
It's a dark night.

It is a dark night—I go back my past
to recall my childhood.
I stay lonely in my room.
I need concentration to fix my mood.

It is a dark night.
I can feel the stillness.
I can feel its importance
Because I have to write.

It is a dark night.
I've just lighted my lamp slightly.
but my future is waiting for me.
I need to make it glorious and bright.

A Dazzling Day

Delightful morning, Fresh air,
White blooming—
and the charming blossoms . . . .
I am in my little garden.
Here I get strength to ease my burdens.

Somebody says us 'good bye'.
Someone just sees
the world with its
New eyes.

So, we should not waste
the beauty of this dazzling day.
We should taste.
We should enjoy.

Oh! God,
You are the ALL.
I am just too kid
to earn my credit.
Sometimes I fail
to maintain your creed.

But I get a new way
for this cheerless life
by the help of such a dazzling day.
Yes, it's really an easeful day.

A Deserted Heart

I bestowed homage to a homelike fellow.
But I got a hollow love.
I tried to show my humbleness, but it was merely a
hulking matter.
She never cared . . . .
I muttered; and I was suffered.
Latter, I considered it like a contemptible prick.
I came to know that, life sometimes might be stood on
the wall of undurable bricks.
Well, I named it—'The emotional brigandage.'

One day I saw a beggar passing by the street.
I went closer to him.
I saw a boldness in his eyes;
Though he was in grief,
But he could easily tolerate his insatiable life.
I became perplexed for while!
Now, my deserted heart attached with a divine
ingrowing infinity.
So, this deserted heart got the veritable dignity (of life)
at last.

A Deserve

A deserve, that makes me happy,
A deserve, that feels me wondrous,
Is the smoother of this wretched mind.
I have become thirsty very much desiring this deserve.
I am always a thought—reader.
But now, I want to become thoughtless in your love.
I want myself to surrender . . .
Thus, I want to be tied with you by this deserve.
I know, you are the tolerant;
And you will not consider me as a troublesome fellow.
So, let' s become THE ONE,
And we shall say, 'Good-bye, to the sorrow.'
We shall see enlightenment tomorrow.

A Feeling

It is a moonlit midnight.
I am with my bare feet.
I have no fright but a little bit delight.
The view is so polite
That It seems the world becoming bright (though in midnight)
I am walking with my shabby brush as to sweep
for a dusty field.
A new cleared ground would appear after the cleansing,
but do you know what is my actual thinking?
I am tempered for your sorrow
because this night may become painful for the coming morrow
for losing something or someone . . .
only a prayer is needed if you can.
It may save from the waste.
So, I do request.
Divinity sometimes provokes me, and
I want to say, I am not single-handed in this singleness stand.
Well, wish be happy everyone in this world.
Now, this charming night is very short.
I shall have to do a lot . . .
I will release myself from the duty I got.
I will again see a night
like such wonderful night.
Such bright night, really a beautiful night!

A Letter From The Heaven

I have heard a note from heaven.
I have nodded my head
as I have to explore it across this world.
I have received a letter.
It says, "The God needs an emendator".
Me, the empty-headed thinks
that It would be a duty of propagandists.
But, the world itself begets propagandists.
The world propagate a theologist.
We all are the tenant of this God gifted world.
Therefore, we need to understand.
I am just a follower not a theorist.
So, I differ myself from the vulgar, majestic optimists.
They just declare,
but they don't make it clear.
We shall have to palliate sorrows but not making only a
proclamation.
We need self-devotion.
That's the revelation.
That's the letter from heaven . . .

A Spring-Afternoon

I am thinking for a walk, and

I just decided to have a walk outside my home.

I am passing by my street.

I am looking at the afternoon's view.

Spring just has arrived . . .

I can smell its essence.

So, I am glad to sensualize it.

But, what does it cost for a senseless?

Now, I can realize the sayings of great men

as too many beautiful songs have been sung in an
orderly manner (to expose the pleasures of spring).

I just met with my closest one,

(My spiritual preceptor)

and shared opinions to bring back again our former
reverence.

I need to collect such wisdom.

It is necessary to cater to these all along.

Now, I am going back home.

Suddenly, I got the disperse of a wonderful day light
and its reflection on a reddish ground and brown clay.

It looks like a heavenly day.

It takes me and my sense out from mournful
contemplation.

I just got a snooty but smooth, still relaxation.

It seems the day wants to be dawn again flushing such
light.

You are Marvelous!

You are glamorous-Spring-afternoon.

It's my fate to manifest you (Spring-afternoon) . . . .

I think, I have reached the extreme edge of my emotion.

I want to compare it with a little dreamy excursion.

It does not happen, but I have it!

I am just observing,

and I feel nothing—but . . . . (I can stick my eyes to see
this afternoon).

I have not enough thoughts to depict.

I shall have to create sentences, but I can't right now.

I will always be waiting to see it again.

Yes, it's unspeakable . . . .

It's unfaded.

It's unforgettable.

Now, I have realized a priceless and vulgar word called 'self-applause'.

Be great and always excuse.

So, you are great, The Spring Afternoon.

Addicted

I am addicted.

I am rejected—

by this world.

I never look back

because I never get back.

for what I desire.

As I have lost everything,

I have nothing.

But, I want to let you know,

sometimes a enthusiastic—deadly soul could be found
in the heap of snow

May he have desire

to become again like a flyer.

He needs only sympathy.

He needs a therapy;

through which his sensation may be out of antipathy.

Yes, I am addicted.

I am rejected.

I want to revive.

Let me survive . . . .

An Untold Story

There is something happened with me.
There is something ignored me.
Life sometimes tells something indiscernible!
Life often recalls a certain and indissoluble thing.
I don't know, why it's indescrible (sometimes).
But must pay attention to it if it becomes a subject of
indignation.
Thus, one could achieve a philosophical doctrine.
So, I am now the introducer of my former pricks.

I was once lacked in prevision.
I was very presumptuous of myself.
A pretty face often knocked and made pretension with me.
My whole sense being spread widely, retained in a
refutation.
I was engaged in a mellifluous tune
Which was very delightful.
But I was plucked from that illusion.
I did not know, how was I glissaded?

Now, I have chosen a different world that starts with a
new day.
That's why, I give you my feelings every day.
I guide my life with soft steps.
I know, my former emotions has gone.
Now, the emotion emitting (from my sense)
Gives me power to write, and I get a sweet essence.
Yes, this is the essence of a empiric life.
It helps me to survive.

Anguish

Mind it friends, everyone has emotion—

But somebody is also suffering in frustration (because of emotion).

We all are seeking its solution,

But don't worry, there is a co-ordination

between frustration and emotion—

which can make a resolution.

(I know it, friends)

There is nothing but a simple devotion.

Just forget all of your ascription,

For what you lost or you would get as an incarnation.

Just keep it in your mind of passion and sensation,

But don't apply it for destruction

Someday you would get it.

And it would have solved with your full gratification.

Be A Poet

Imagination, thought, embodiment

and at last praiseworthy comments.

I know these all need a poet,

You see, a commendable guerdon is flowing from the past for them.

Now, I am looking at everyone's tradition.

Yes, all are genius.

I see, some were furious,

and always took part to sacrifice themselves.

Some were serious, and used to ruminate themselves.

Dignity kissed their faces.

But tell me, why did such two devastative incidents occur (in the same century) ?

Manifestation of mankind has rolled more than a thousand year,

and how can you say? . . . .

"The third may not occur."

Power and the chair of sentiment don't care of you at all.

They only know how to tramp and make radiation.

So, I don't care, who is going to take the lordship,

And who would accept the dictatorship.

I know, most of us don't care.

But those who cares must extol.

So, be a poet.

Be a poet . . .

Please, don't deviate.

Bewildered

Bewildered !
I'm just bewildered.
love once blessed me.
and I adorned it with my best.
Bewildered!

This contrite mind followed every single moment
caring of you.
Such huge was the hug (and my deepest thoughts) !
It could be felt as a current
which would perish all my sins.
Even, it was supposed to be a soulful image dressed with
profundity.
It made an inseparable integrity.

But now, I am a loser and missed my identity.
I just failed to presignify . . . .
if I did so,
I might be saved pressing my sense and my immatured
sensibility.
Bewildered!
I'm just bewildered . . . .

Bleeding

Bleeding from eyes,

And bleeding from my heart—

I don't care . . .

But I do dare.

I took the revolution as an inseparable part in my life.

I was placed under the custody.

But I never felt humble myself, and I will not lose my agony.

I fight for my friends, my 'LOUTISH FRIENDS'—

And I will be fighting for them until the system will be allowed to become balanced.

You see, I always keep my patience.

But don't try to fidget me.

Don't try to aggravate my revolutionary sense.

The tyrant crown will be diminished.

They must retrocede.

You will see a reversal (a new era).

You will welcome it.

But bleeding . . .

Yes, this is a gladsome bleeding.

This is an inviolate, but an irresistible bleeding.

Blind Mind

To love you
is to be a fortunate one.
The sense to feel your heart
Wants always to be with you.
May your sentiment
do not want to allow such attachment.
But believe me,
I am so curious to know your deepest sense.
Let me know whether it is wrong or right.
After all, you are the same as you were before
for this blind mind.

Confession

I write

and I can also fight.

I fight for injustice.

I fight for sarcastic

and mislead of your mentality (incapability to fight for injustice).

I am the protector of a devout,

at the same time, I bend my head in front of a scout.

You will see a' spark.'

A spark, which is unbeatable

because something is going intolerable . . . .

You say, 'Humanity is a gift of the God.'

Yes, that's right.

So, I want to fight

for what gone to unfair.

Manpower has been corrupted in every layer (most of us are selfish).

To die before death

is no doubt great

for those who the fellow of regret.

Ear-less will never realize it.

Thereby, I shall have to fight.

Please stand by me,

and, we shall again see

a prestigious, theistic world . . . . ,

Yes, this is me. (but I am a simple and well—tempered boy)

Cursed

Ten days have passed,
But still bleeding and bleeding . . .
Parents crying have no ideas; they says, "Cursed".
I am laughing . . . . but,
It's not a joy.
I am laughing at my mistake.
Everyone's heart has been exasperated.
A prayer, a prayer, a prayer . . . .
I call my lord, please save me.
It has been caused
because something has been lost.
But, this pain is more awful than that loss.
It was enforcing me to be drowned into a false.
A false!
I have got everything and it's reflecting before my eyes.
The most impressive I see now is the parental love.
Now, I have come to know, the paramount motive
should be (in my life) to repay this love.
It can reduce the toxin from my body.
It can be haematic to stop my face becoming bloody.
Oh! God, please save me . . . .
I will never do the same happing with me (as this is the
cause of bleeding)
I will devote myself to the service of good ceremony
and I don't want to hear again such painful melody.
It's cursed . . . .
Now, I've understood the harmfulness addiction of drug.

Delighted

Oh! God, life is such!

Full of joy and much . . .

But, somebody says, 'there are too many grief, in the heart of life'.

While, I say, 'see it in the core of your heart which is same as an oasis of desert'.

Sorrow may come in every moment and term,

For what you have lost, and

It has been paid for no cost!

So, life is mazy,

playful, unbounded, misty and crazy.

Moment goes and moment comes . . .

And, when you will gather all your desire in sum,

You would find,

Why so curious and anxious was my mind?

Then, you would say, 'Why my mind was full of palpitation'?

And, You may say, 'Everything should get its suitable,
(time) for what It gets the solution,

And—It's worthless to mourn for such condition.

So, It's none but me,

And I am lucky one to be a part of that situation.

Ha! the world is funny,

And I proud to be a member of my own destiny,

Oh! God.

Destination

Everyone has a destination,
And I want to fly . . . .
I want to hide behind the clouds
And want to be an unallied (just for fun).
I want to reach,
At the end of an unknown beach.
Where I could be free from the fury.
I want to see endmost and endless (view).
I don't want to be encircled.
My sensibilities should not be enclasped
I wish to enter into a ritualistic kingdom,
And it should be fenceless.
Just come at my beautiful world.
It may be colorful for those, you are still suffering for
being unclean and uncolored.
You think it's an uncanny and must be a joke!
But I have to unclose.
Yes, I have to unclose . . . .
It's my destination,
And I have to encroach.

Divine Grace

Life, sometimes falling and sometimes rising,
is full of various sensations.
I beg sometimes for a divine grace.
It helps me to be strong at every stage.

Now, I am sitting on the top of wall
Which separates the sea from the city.
It make me to be more curious
because it can't protect if this huge watery earth starts to
show its calamitous tendency.

So, my Lord be with me.
I always want to fulfill ebullient wishes, and I am like
those falling and rising waves.
but I respect your kingdom—
I bend my head in front Thou, and I worship Thee.

Does A Poet Write Only For The Poets?

I want to be a poet.
I want to explore my thoughts through my poetic sweat.
You know, freedom is the basic need of commons.
A poet always maintains this through his words of
commiseration.
Even a child can pronounce a rhyme!
It's a poet's harmonic act that controls every line.
Sometimes a poet exceeds his speech making
exaggerations.
An audience (of any class) should presume it by his
prevision.
Though a poet makes a class,
But all classes need a poet.
So, tell me—does a poet only write for the poets?

Foreign Birds

Holding my pen in right hand
I am just thinking
and invoking the words.
Sometimes I write few lines
and sometimes I stopped.
Thus.my inner sense is falling
and after some time it's rising.

Suddenly, my eyes caught
a team of foreign birds.
I do not know about their class.
Their wings are multicolored and full of slush.
I am unknown to their destiny.
But I know they are free.
They know no barriers,
They are not like us.
We make encirclement.
We make barrage from each other.
We are not free like those foreign birds.

Forgive and Forget

They say forgive and forget,
I am in touch of you yet.
I am still confused.
What is it about,
Love or a little kindness?

I gave you my heart.
You took it like a flirt.
I was about to achieve my goal,
and you played a player's role.
But i was still in touch with you.

Now, I stay alone but want to win your heart (not
your . . .).
I have made my own faithful path.
This will cure my feelings you wanted to hurt.
This will be great—
to forgive you and forget.

From That Day . . . .

I woke up in that morning.

I saw a nice view of nature outside the window.

I wanted to feel the day.

I wanted to explore my perceptions from that day.

I used to sit beside my little (but beautiful) garden.

I used to try to share something marvelous like them.

I used to write few words to impress you like them.

They are the noble-minded.

Me, a muddy boy always took my sense and my endurance at leisure.

Now, I came to know,

They always tried to show the actual law to reduce the drawback of life.

Yes, they were truly the lettered.

So, I got a lesson—

And I wanted to impress you by their admonitions

From the day.

Yes, from that day.

I always remember it (that day) before starting a rendition.

It was a remarkable and a resplendent day.

Haven Of The Heaven

We can't see the land's figure perfectly staying in the
middle of sea,
And you never feel the prevision of an adventurous
sailing being a landlocked
The sky never shows its end.
Our untamed emotions always looking for a new
happening.
There are no bondages of our feelings.
We always live for a hope.
There is no end of the era.
One comes and other goes.
You can't make an agreement in a good fellowship.
It knows only to sacrifice.
It always pours a lasting essence of peace.
So, be a large-minded.
Curiosities never get tired.
They are the brother of earnestness.
We never betrayed by the moment.
We just need to catch its intention.
We are only the strangers for next day's performance
and situation.
We can buy the earth-born materials by our earnings
except the morality.
There is no fullness of imagination,
And it always remains hungry for a new good
sensational perception.
You can't latch it.
You can't fend it.
We all always have to prove a new excellence to get a
new exaltation.

So friends, this is our indecipherable World.
But, it's really unspeakable and decorous!
It's itself a haven for the godliness and heaven.
Oh! My hand is now weary.
I need rest,
And I am going to attain a festal fete.

He Will Come

He knows the song.
The song of sympathy.
He will take away your sorrows
So that you can sing a sweet religious song.

He only wishes to provoke your sense,
And he wants your good judgments.
Thus, he can save us from the bondage.
We must have to fight against the offence.

Then he will sing a song.
He will show the love
Which is endless and permanent.
He needs to come.

Just pray so that he can freely come.
He is an unique, delightful
And handsomer than the handsomest.
So, Just wait—and let him come.

Believe me, he must come.
He is the hope of a hopeless prisoner.
He will diminish the paroxysm.
He will finish the persecution.

Heavenly Thoughts

Sweet thoughts, bright face,
Cheerful days,
Huge ambitions,
Permanent relaxation
Through deep contemplation,
to perceive great ideas
by meditation—
It seems, all are going to be sunk
beyond this life full of worthless
and vague material needs.
I do not want to bind myself for such deeds.
Lying on a grassy field
My inmost consciousness
Tries to provoke the rightful sense.
So, I pray to my God
Please help me to get back my boldness
and earlier valuable, germinating
and heavenly thoughts.
This life already has taught me a lot.
Only the darkness I can see now
and sorrows till now I have got.

Helpless

I am a helpless fellow.
But I dream of a sweet day, and it will be mellow.
I have had my mysterious thoughts as a companion.
It will work between me and the world as a mediation.
I know, I will not be sympathized.
I know, I will never get back my personality as a
perpetual and recognized.
My Lord says, "Act for right justice as a proud
through which you can make your sentence loud."
My perceived sense from seminary will go for vulgar
If I stay vouching wrong deeds longer.
So, I need to be stronger.
Though I am a helpless,
but someday you can see a charming fondness from this
helpless.

I Have Left The Door Of Glory And Praise

I have left the door of glory and praise.
I just think of my memoirs.
I've just got a meed.
Yes, my name has been chosen from the heap of hatred.
But I want to be a suitor for those poor-houses.
I want to share their agony.
I know their untamed indignation
Because they live in indignity.
I am now an indissoluble part of such community.
I have no regard for my own individuality.

I want to share your pang
When you miss your betrayer,
Loose all—and release your suspense.
This world is beautiful, and we need not to squabble.
Spurn all spurious bonds.
These are the cause of scourge.
These are scorching.
We have to sustain . . .
We shall earn the self-consciousness.
So, I have left the hall of recompense,
I have left the door of glory and false praise.

I Miss You

Heart breaks
as I miss you.
Each day ends,
and I miss you.

Soul becomes dry and is out of fancy
as I miss you.
Your face makes fervency
as I miss you.

I want to be a forbearant—
I fail to be so
as I miss you.
Yes, I miss you.

Sometimes I pretend
to be an arrogant.
But I do not know, what should I do?
I know nothing as I still miss you.

Love gives me the pain (again).
I am not so skillful to maintain (this pain).
I need you.
Believe me, I miss you . . . .

I Swear

I swear, I swear.
I am not a betrayer.
I am out of fear.
I swear.
As a real admiration,
does not need any false reiteration.
I get too many inspirations
and I am told to follow so many directions.
But I just take the real perceptions
Which would help us to adopt the indecomposable
(and unique)
Truth and morality.
I know those are the indissolvable part of divinity.
thus, we still maintain humanness and civility.
I swear—
I am not a liar.

I Want To Regain My Love

The greatest moment of this life,
which is unspeakable and inexplicable,
is to achieve such temperance without any lamentation.
I feel much better than my past.
Now I can feel a silent flow of a mystical lesson,
but it is very workable for me.
I lost the mobility of this life, but I didn't lose the
mnemonic part
which helped me to prepare for the next.
My neighbors and my friends were mocking at me
because it was insufficient to establish a moat against
this wrong mobocracy.
Later I changed its mode.
Even my love made mistrust upon me!
Yet I was living for a hope.
I didn't want to know its effect.
My mind was retarded
by the bad influence at that time.

However, I have resuscitated my sense at last.
Now being a reticent fellow,
I try to devalue those invaluable facts.
A lineage or a race is not enough for me. So, I've chosen
this world,
and I have to share a lot.
Yes, I will share.
I want to regain my love.

I Want To Regain My Love (Part-2)

I was about to tell you,

But I was lost in my words.

I was bound in critical circumstances.

Now, I can smell a sweet essence of excitable, joyous life.

(and i can see the ideal image of love)

I feel the largeness, and I feel the(heavenly) relief.

You see, I always mention some hypothetical phrases.

But don't take it as a disgusting reiteration.

Please, don't forget me.

I know, it is intolerable . . . .

But you are only mine.

It's just a short missing!

I can restore myself by your euphony.

Sometimes I like to evade.

Yes, it's funny.

But, you are mine.

It is an evolvement.

Yes, the evolvement of our true LOVE—

The figure, I have drawn in my memory is same as i see
in my real eyes—

And it's only you!

Isn't it a real love?

I Wish To Meet With You Again

Two hearts once met with each other.
They talked to each other.
It was felt like a gracious moment,
For few seconds.
Emotion came, and mingled a miracle.
They wanted it to enjoy.
It was a moment of faith and unspeakable joy.
But, latter it was surrounded by deceitfulness.
They considered each other like a false-hearted.
The moment had been left desert
Before being famed.
The fallacy was caused by a drossy pride.

But now, the pride is distressing their sense.
Temporal intimacy should not be so tenuous.
To leave a sinless mind and a well-wisher is an idiot's
offence.
They are still waiting to meet again.
Will they have it (again) ?

I Wrote Your Name

I wrote your name in the book of my own life—history.
I sorted your face to cling it on the cover of my first page.
You were one of tremendous part of my life-story.
Once the morning started viewing your tactful face.
Yes, your beautiful face.

But now, these all want to be free and crack gradually.
It could be priceless even without caring me.
It would be a part of your gladness.
It may cheer you up as you want to be a thoughtless.
Now, I am thinking a little bit,
To have a sort trip for my country-side
Where I could find some liveliness and gaiety.
I know only the nature stays my friend and can
counterpoise my last felicity.
But, I did write your name in the book of my own
life—history.

If I could have flown in the sky, I would have been a messenger of humanity.

If I had been in the powerful strength to dedicate, I would have destroyed the insincerity.

If I had had a true friend, I would have sung a song of dignity.

If I were a patriot, I would have conquered everyone's heart being a part of the delicate community.

If I could have dispersed the delineation of spirituality, I would have filled up the necessity of human deficiency.

If I had cried truly and heartily in front of You, my Lord; I would have surely perished the scarcity (of divinity).

If I could have been allowed to proceed to fight for establishing tranquility,

I would have tried my utmost to remove the trashy sovereignty.

Oh! my beloved friends, can you hear the sound (emerging from the stream of heaven) ?

If yes, then keep your attitude strong and bound.

Ill-Fated

How can I tell you?
How can I impress you?
My worthless feelings tremble to expose it in front of you.
Though I am so much rueful, but tell me-How can I rue?
Now, It is not that face which once used to share glisten
of love with you.

There is no certainty, but by God! I've been able to
touch the eternity.
I know, it's difficult to get the warm dignity (though
being silent lover).
So, it hurts me and I have to take deep breath.
Now, I am holding a pen to recall my past and the
prosody to be entitled.
I will not say it again.
I will not make an iteration.
Everyone is decent.
Everyone is an intemperate.
Though I am going to be an ill-fated,
But a lot of intellects I have to collect.
I want to be a moderate.

In Disguise

I stay in disguise.
I have to talk through only my eyes.
I relinquish my desires because I cause pains to
someone.
I forbid myself to make remedies.
I've been a fellow of castigation.
Only God can save me . . . .
My story might be listed in the book of futility.
But this will not harm anyone.
I need an everlasting solemnity.
Then, I can feel a good turn, and I would be a messenger
again of serenity.
So, please help me,
and forgive me if I hurt someone by those words.
Donoy worry, I am in disguise.

Inspiration

I am watching a skylark

flying skyward.

It's famous for its song.

I am sitting here, on the top of a wall, and

thinking . . . .

What is my actual liking?

I have spent too much time with my colleagues.

I have had my periods with relatives.

I like very much some of them.

But, Alas! I am still the same.

Whatsoever, now, I am watching a tiller.

He spends his time to make us survivor (in this world).

Many poets have supplicated prayer to God for them

as they are the bearer of living-flow.

But, I am not a tiller.

I want to do something similar.

I will do the second thing

which is needful for a human being.

I will teach the glorious and heavenly lesson to mankind.

Thus, I may become like the skylark, and then

I would fly thoughtlessly and hourly like the skylark.

Last Prayer

Dead . . .
He is dead.
He left us.
He left his two little daughters.
He is now surrounded by his well-wishers.
It's a mournful day.
He wanted to be with us,
But did not stay.

The youngest (of his daughters) does not know,
What ritual is going to bestow
To his father.
She is just kissing her father's cheeks.
We know what she still seeks.
She only knows he is her father.
Oh! my God, I know,
You make our fate.
We just surrender us to you.
There is no secret.

After all his my elder cousin.
He is no more.
We have to pray the last farewell song.
We want you to stay in heaven
Which is peaceful but very long (from us).
God bless you.
Please God give him again a joyful life
Without any material grief.

Little Traveler

I woke up in that morning.
I guessed it would be pleasant day.
I felt its freshness.
the wind was blowing sweetly and slowly.
I began to enjoy it with the sense of glee.

I later became to think about my duties
Which had to be fulfilled by the day.
So many burdens I got, I had to fill up
Though my soul wanted to be in touch
with such beautiful for little while.

I had managed my breakfast
before i went to outside to solve my task.
I saw a little bird
making noise in front of my windows.
Its wings were soft and fully colored.

It was looking at me—
I loved its style
by which it was winking at me—
and I too doing the same thing.
I became an addict (in it) for some time.

I thought if you and me would be
the dwellers of the same world,
We would become free
from all cares.
We would only make love and there would be no hurry.

So, good bye little traveler.
I said, 'you are free,
You know no boundary;
and let me go back to my own world
Full of misery'.

Loneliness

Heart breaks in loneliness.
A frosty morning; daylight repeals it, and I feel loneliness
on the eve of the day.
When it rains,
a swallow wants to denote a song.
But, after that world calls loneliness.
I see the river flowing, and I come closer to the bank.
I heard the river roaring more in loneliness.
When I stay in my study room
thinking past events, my conscience becomes more
powerful in loneliness.
It's better to stay sometimes in loneliness.
We need sometimes to alleviate pains in loneliness.
You see, love often adorns more homage in loneliness.
Loneliness . . . .
When a war ends,
It becomes time to return for soldiers in loneliness;
and we all mourn in loneliness.
Then we realize what peace is!
One day we all have to say the world 'good bye' in
loneliness.
Yes, loneliness . . . .

My Last Days

How will be my last days?
Depressed, deserted or thoughtless . . .
if i do something wrong,
It can't be compensated, and
It will be too long.

But God i pray thee—
Forgive me
If you see something sinful in me.
I want to rest.
I want to be a messenger of THE GRACE.
Please forgive me
and make colorful and bright my last days.

My Love

Can you hear me?
You can't because you have chosen this incongruent world.
Can you feel me?
You can't because you are merely a part of incontinence.
Can you love me?
You can't because you are just a liar.
Can you respect me?
You can't because you hate the penury.

But I can feel the truth appearing vividly in my heart.
So, I want to destroy this rigorous love running after you.
I do not want to be drowned into incivility.
I respect the purity.
I want THE LOVE inclined towards divinity.
Then I shall embellish myself freely.

My New Poem

My new poem is about my reveal of my life's strain.
My new poem is like my newly conceived brain.
Yes, I want to write these feelings through my poem.
I say frequently, "I would hanker after for a painful
materialistic, egoistic love."
But it has become totally changed.
Now, I can compare my thoughts between bluff and love.

I never count, how many seasons have passed?
But I do recollect my past
for resurrecting myself from dust.
Only I was shocked
as I was a fellow of lack of sense, and my sensitive mind
was blocked.

Now, I can feel the frenzy wind.
I have got a restored mind.
So, I am capable to write my new poem.
Now, I am proceeding with enormous joy.
I want myself to employ
for to remove your frustration
by the help of friendly condescension.
Then, we all will enjoy.
We will make a moment of greatest joy.
This is my new poem.

My Pen Does not Want to Wait

My pen does not want to wait.
My pen does not want to stop.
The pen has a faith
because I am his friend.

So, I am praying to my God,
Bless me with your grace
by which I can make my readers happy;
and there will be the loveliness in everyone's face.

A day goes away and another will come.
In this way, I also wish;
My new thoughts should come one by one.
Oh! God please help me to embellish.

My pen does not want to delay.
Time is very important.
Once it's gone, there will be no way.
So, my pen does want to make delay.

Oh, God please accept my pray.
I can do nothing without your grace.
Give me the force, so that I can write some suitable phrase.
Yes, I need your grace.

Obligation

My heart is going on,

And I do not want to delay long.

I shall have to sing too many life-songs.

Sometimes I think, a misty morning

Full of sweet longing,

Would dispel all the day's sorrow;

And I may reach the crest of the world tomorrow.

Sincerity is my strength, curiosity is my nature.

Oh! God, I know you are the sketcher, inventor and nominator . . . .

Nobility is not a friend of miser.

So, I have to sing a lot of song;

And it is the duty of every young.

Oh! God Bless Me

It's raining slowly and silently
and the night is silent (too).
I am trying to invigorate
My poetic feelings at this moment.
But my words loose the exact meaning,
They can't touch my inmost sense.
They are failing to commemorate.
The words are not coming out.
But it's an exact time to send this world a holy message.
Oh! God help me please.
Only you can give me a consecrate
and a meaningful substance.
I think the rain will not stop
as this is your desire.
You are almighty
We do not know your intense.
So, my Lord please bless me.
Give me a sweet sense.
I am ready to wait
because it's very hard to become a good poet.
Oh! God bless me.

Our Wordsworth

Oh! Wordsworth, Oh! Wordsworth . . . .
We are still in debt to you, and we will have to be.
You enhanced the strength of poetry.
You made a marvelous tune to enrich poetry.
Oh! Wordsworth . . . .
We can now clarify our thoughts with extend because of
you, Wordsworth.
You euphonized poetry without the indenture—but
with moderation,
and it's decorous.
This will be evergreen, and everlasting.
It's a mnemonics and I always follow it.
Oh! Wordsworth . . . .

Outburst Of Emotion

My emotion took outburst when I had spent few hours
in my brother's marriage ceremony hall.
You know, I prefer more to stay alone.
By the way, all (my cousins, my uncles, my
nephews . . . .)
were compiling that special moment.
Some were gladdening to girt me as I met them after a
long period at all.
But me, the same . . . .
My two lips were just the giver of charming cheap smile.
I was much comfortable sitting on a chair,
and I was not able to share.
Suddenly, a call!
I heard a call.
Babai . . . . (my nick name)
I was requested to take few shots.
My one of closest cousins said, "Please take a shot, now
we all are in company".
He said, "Who does know,It would be same tomorrow?"
Yes, I did it.
I took so many snapshots.
I took that speech as simple.
But now, I can feel friends what it (the call) was!
I can't but embarrass with tears.
You know, I am bearing lot of pains.
Sometimes an inexpressible moment stains.
I also want to keep moments to be stabilized.

But what can I do? ? ?
Too many arrangements will have to be done . . . .
So, I have to spend my life in a standing stale lodge
(bearing such unforgettable moments)
I have to . . . .
I have to . . . .

Please Come Back

I used to sit by the bank of the river flown by the side of
my countryside;
And I saw one day, so many kinds of stream (with many
different shapes) going towards their destination.
But they never came back.
They will never come back!

I used to watch on the sky and see the postures of
clouds—
Suddenly these were vanished.
The exact portraits never came back.
I know, they will not . . . .

You see, if human revelation once falls under the wreck,
It's very hard to restore its attributions.
The benefaction for a community never comes back.
Yes, it doesn't come back.

But you, special then a commoner holding my worldly
senses, must come back.
I always miss you . . .
You have to come back.
Please come back.

Please Come Back (Part-2)

Come back,
My dear, please come back.
I have made a sweet anthology from my soul.
I have created a new tune.

I will bestow you this passionate heart.
I think—you would too pay reverence
As love needs regard.
Let's reunite.

Pain comes and it may cause reversion
Again!
But we will have to swear,.
We will ignore little faults.
We will never err.

Let's celebrate our reunion.
I shall make an euphony for your reception.
I shall trace a beautiful sign of our love.
My dear, please come back.

Priceless Beauty

My cup is being poured with tasteful liquor of tea.

A prominent face comes gradually in front of me.

So many commitments have been proclaimed by
him(for the sake of our society)

I'm just here to consign a request politely.

Of course, I must as he is an executive of our society.

So, I am being served with a cup of tea.

Now, I said to him, 'Sir, we need several activities

As the slam dwellers are being suffered from
servility-only your executive power can diminish.'

Though He knows about the calamities,

But he don't want to surcease.

Therefore, I got a clement smile,

and a response, 'No'.

He just shows his pride.

He just explores his parade.

He is just a glib.

Now, I have to go back with grieves.

I couldn't fetch a hope, and pleasure on their faces like
dry petal leaves.

A man, I think, becomes a beast

When two reasons I'm going to enlist (for it).

Firstly, he might be a dreamless

Like a day surmounts in sunless,

And the last one can be attributed for those who have
become heartless.

You know, we greet those fellows.

We nod our heads in front of those fellows.

Yes, they are the heartless.

They are only to radiate luxuries.

They hurt me exposing their self-acquired beauties.

I think, It's an absurd gravity.

Therefore, I call it, priceless beauty.

Purity

Tears drop from my eyes.
Shall I compare it with a dew-drop?
A dew-drop!
It's a refresher.
It gives a strength to our mind,
It brings a new feeling.
When I see it, I forget my missing.
Have you any doubt for its purity?
But the drops shedding from my eyes also says, 'I am pure, watch it,
think it and feel it.'
Yes, grief is the part a mournful fellow tortured by a tormentor.
I can smell its flavor.
A mild heart exposes its righteousness by these drops of tear.
Now, I have learned to sacrifice
as I am a human being not a device.
I have feelings.
Yes, now, I can see something more into a dew-drop.
I can meditate the similarity
between tears and dew-drops.
I know about the purity.
I am not a pursuivant of misanthropy.

Restless

If I share my earlier days,
you may taste it with your joyous mind.
some of them may not take it as serious.
I know, everyone has a different value of sense.
but something has made me blind.

I am just faithless—
about my love, about my passion . . .
though my soul is strong enough,
but my sense and my intellectual strength are restless.
yet I hope, LOVE would be an occasion
once again.
(yes, again . . .)

She Is So Proud

She is so proud.
She is so dispassionate.
She shirks me,
But I get glee.

She is so proud.
She hates me,
And I have no doubt.
She feels herself stout.

She is so proud.
She thinks-she is out of agony.
I like it and
Her style of expressing serenity.

She is so proud.
But I've got her nerves—the hollowness may make her
starved.
She will miss me
Someday, and she would again feel that love she once
deserved.

Sometimes

Sometimes I fail to find the words.
Sometimes I can not perceive the exact feelings.
So, sometimes I hesitate to write down my verse.
Sometimes I get the emotion—
But I lose it at once.

Sometimes there is a conflict
Making the lines of love in this mind—
But I do not retreat.
So, sometimes I succeed—
and lastly I make some lines sweet and poetic.

I know life is short—
and the times to feel (to fly in emotions)
are too short.
Therefore, I do not want to wait more,
I need to escort.
(with you my friends).
Yes, my friends . . .

Sometimes a Word Gets More Powerful Meaning

He said to you,
'You are forever mine'.
It's a simple word—
even a careless fellow
Utters it easily and tactfully.

But it becomes a serious speech
When he becomes to keep up his promise—
And he is ready to face to show its actual meaning.
Yes, we all know he will not retreat;
He will always maintain the feeling.

But she takes it merely like a loving word of passion.
She knows how to treat it.
She owes her beauty.
It's very costly.
Though he not only likes her face,
But also he finds something
Which is more precious
Than your face.
So, he said to you, 'Forever mine'.

Sometimes I Get Emotion

'Salvation' and I need it.
I always fight for the wrong.
So, I sing directly suggesting song.
Insinuation is not liked by me.
I compare it to insincerity.
An ostentatious heart is always excited to see
The end line of the eternity.
But, is it possible?
You will say, "no".
A right thing should not be suppressed
On the eve of new movement.
We need only devotion
and give it an essence of right emotion.
Now, You would say, "Yes,
and It is in control of our sense".
So, you and me (We) all need salvation . . . .
To make the world out of calamitous sensation.
That's why, sometimes I get emotion.

Song

Oh! God, give me a song
To fight for the wrong.
Though you have given me a tongue,
But I am not so strong
To manage, to unite, to drown.
I have come almost to the edge, and
I am ready to face;
I am going to trace the tract
Of human-toxin.
But, Oh! God, give me the power;
Give me a song.
I want to make morality stay long.
Give me a song.
Give me a song . . . . Oh! God.

Spring, You Are Amazing

Too many springs
have passed.
Each spring brings a new hope.
I want full relaxation,
I want to get back my past feelings.

Spring after spring;
I still wait, and I will be waiting . . .
(Spring) the season full of love,
I am waiting to see your face
Oh! my beloved.

Too many springs
have passed . . . .
My love is still unstained.
Though my mind is unstable,
But my love will be the same.

I know, spring, You are full of sweetness.
Please get me back my love.
Make me a fortunate.
I will not give up the hope, I will wait.
Spring . . . . You are amazing!
Yes, You are amazing . . . .

Storm

I saw a storm last night.

It was surrounding and uplifting the earth.

I saw it frightening the land and its crops.

It seemed that the land was allowing it (the storm) to make a huge cavern.

I know, this is its nature.

I know, it palpitates our hearts.

But, I want to tell you something friends.

Who could visualize the storm causing pain inside my mind and my soul?

Only my friendly and undetached feelings can reach to it.

I could be released if it (the storm ruling inside my heart) would be wash out by last night's storm.

Then, I could feel a fresh frenzy touch

Slowly and sensuously ceasing blood.

But don't worry, friends.

I am not a rough.

I can feel the blindness in love.

Though I am suffering to live in a disgusting port,

but I still have a hope.

My emotion takes me sometimes out of control.

That's why, I call it storm.

Strange

I like to write loving words.
I write it
and I share it.
Sometimes I manage a project,
but I inform its form
Before it's completed.
Sometimes I guess the word
to which I want to decorate,
but it becomes a different one
with a new sense.
I am too little to establish the exact instances.
Though I try to control my words,
but it's very strange to right a verse.
I do not know my sense
as it changes its mood.
I do not know, what will be the next?
Really strange . . .
Very strange . . . .

Summer Dream

It's winter.
We all are enjoying it.
The morning starts with full plate of toasts, breads and
a cup of tea or coffee(whatever you like).
Well, I am sitting by the window—it is a showery day
of winter.

Suddenly my perceptions (both physical and inner
sensation) take me to feel a shiny day of last summer!
Now, I can see the brightness and boldness of the sea
standing alone at the seashore.
Sweat wets my body and I am ready to have fun with
the tides.
Sometimes I become expletive crazy to play with the sea.
Sometimes I get such emotions which is inexplicable.
Sometimes I consider the day as unawares worthy.
But now, it's winter!
Oh! I've just shuffled myself in a dream (day-dream)
Yes, it was a dream.

But it was amazing!

The summer is dancing in front of my eyes in a cloudy
winter morning.

I named it 'The Summer Dream'.

Sweet and Pleasing

The merriment to love you . . . ,
I know your soul is bound for me;
and I am for you.
I think it's the meritorious part of my life.
I can merrily perish the grief.

It's long—I have seen your beautiful eyes,
Your moderate smile
and your charming, mesmeric style.
Those still follow me
Though I am now a wandering man.

we don't know
When we shall again be the same.
We do not know, what will be THE NEXT?
Yet I feel mildness in my heart.
It is like a sweet and pleasing perception to quench my
thirst.

Tell Me, Why?

Tell me, why did once we desire each other?

I never felt emptiness in my mind.

Yes, it was our love!

Why did we use to share a harmonious incommunicable beck.

Tell me?

Why did I use to adorn myself—and why did I use to try my utmost to make a gleam of my love for those days?

It was a true love!

It was such a glorious era that could erase easily one's gloom.

I lived in calmness, and my suitable dreams were about to bloom.

Now, the present time is full of wounds.

I have worthily destroyed my worthless past.

You don't worry.

We both are free . . .

You have to earn for future-and you are undoubtedly illustrious wealth of this earth.

Now, everyone hurts my feelings.

It's hurtful for me.

Me, the lonesome have to live for only to relish the hunger, and to recall my past a little bit.

Tell me, why?

Tell me?

Thank You

I say—thank you.
When I look back my past, I say—thank you.
You know, an optimistic mind always wants to see a
dream (sweet dreams).
Even it could be an undreamt, but he dares to imagine.
Thank you-because you were then a part of this dream.
You cared of my emotions.
You cared of my thoughts.
You got my esteem.
I got love, but it is now something.
Yes, something!
Something, that harasses me now.
It will become a meaningless
I also want to exacerbate it anyhow.
Now, I want to know the exactness.
The exactness that will care for the humanity.
The exactness that will fight for the delinquency.
So, I am anxious a little bit.
But I am not an apathetic.
Good-bye sweet dreams.
Good-bye—and thank you.

The Game

Please listen—
I always hear heart breaking hard tunes.
Each line offers my respect to my love.
Each line sounds my dedication.
But now these thoughts sometimes smile upon me.
Today i am too busy to bring my verses forward.
So, now i take some sad and melancholic tunes as a help
to finish my lines.
You can't make a blame.
I know you are so beautiful,
And you are an innocent.
But you, the first one who played the game.
I was only the part of it.
Now, it's very hard to see its end.
I have lost all my strength.
Only those tunes are my friend.
But i still wish to hold your hands.
I want to please my holy love.
I want again to be the part of the game—
But do not blame me again.

The World Is Huge

The world is huge to feel!
The world is huge to see!
Only a curious one can realize it.
I think, I am little one to justify it,
Because too many time has been wasted for being a
sybarite.
But, now, I have come to know—
That it's very hard to walk barefoot in snow.
The same thing, I have realized for those
Who have suffered a lot before my eyes, and they are my
too close.
So, the world is huge . . .
And I will try my utmost to reduce,
The sadness of ugliness.
Soon it must be a day out of profaneness.

The World is Huge
(Part-2)

I am walking on the road,
Green paddy fields situating by both of sides of it,
Green and green everywhere;
It's very hard to see the ending line—
I stop, I see and I am got perplexed for some time.

I am walking lonely in a desert
Striking the sand by
My legs sometimes
Just for fun.
It is a great joy feeling in my heart.

I am sitting at a beach
Taking delicious fruit juice.
I can see a little ship coming towards the bank.
Does it have any message to encourage me?
As my mind is lack of rapture, it already has become blank.

Sometimes I get too much pains
as I have lost my emotions,
Yet I am not fully destroyed.
I feel, I can write few words and I can muse.
After all, The World is Huge!

To Bind Forever

To love,
To sacrifice,
To bestow,
To dedicate,
To sympathize,
To be a passionate,
To be an intimate;
Everybody knows,
Who own those qualities
are The Fortunate . . . .

I am still in search of a lover
like that.
But I need the grace of the God—
to make myself complete
And to bind her (love) forever.

To Glorify

Hello! Friends, I have to say something
Which I've gathered after thinking and thinking . . .
Too many and countless merits I know.
All have their own inner glow.
But—I think, all are great.
Admiration can never be the same for all except,
a group of people who work only for our gratification and
They are ready to face for every situation.
The world remembers them.
They tell but they try their uttermost to do.
This is their commendable virtue.
This world is for them, however,
sometimes we may forget their contributions,
but we must recall them at the time of revolution.
Lastly, I do not want to tell more about them.
I will always respect them . . . .
I will always glorify them.

To Visualize

Oh! my lord, the shining sun,
Oh! the beautiful hills,
The cheering blue sky—
You always decorate this earth
With precious ornaments, magnificent colors.
Thus, this world is awarded by ever green fields.

Me, a wanderer visit those every single moment
To embellish my temperament.
As I have been defeated by my wish,
She has left me alone.
She was my beautiful lady.
Now, just the false pride (of life) makes her greedy.

Oh! my lord, the shining sun, the master of this earth,
Please give me the strength.
I will dedicate this life
To be a wise—
And making everyone happy,
And i will give the real view to visualize.

Voices For Freedom

We like restoration.
the restoration of arts, of a community
Could solve the deficiency.
the deficiency, Iam taking about, is the forbidden voices
for the freedom.

But I always respect some characters, some memories—
because of their skillful tendency towards holy thoughts.
They are great, and God praises their stories.
So, we need restoration but not dusty libelous summary.

I respect such voices which are odic but not odious.
They merely write some noisome earthly prose.
We don't need these to access.
So, friends the forgotten inspiring tunes will be restored
again because the omnipresent God is with us.

We have to Empower Our Literacy

Love, respect and the worship—
All these are the part to empower literacy.
Everyday a new fellow is born to invent.
We all respect them and want to stretch our hands for
friendship
As we need the strong efficacy
to empower our literacy.

If we look back the past,
too many ways, views and intentions had been cast.
We got Churchill, Virgil, Shakespeare,
Wordsworth . . . . and some of my country-poets.
They had the power to extol.
So, we need to amplify those valuable, encouraged and
everlasting contributions.
After all, my friends, we have to empower the literacy.

We Just Enjoy

A plough-man seeds to make our appetite demolish,
but we just enjoy.
A soldier devotes his life,
and spends all his momentous periods to save our life.
Do you know, how much he has grief?
But, we just enjoy.
A clergyman stays in a hall of sanctification,
and spends more time chanting hymns.
He just wants to see us delighted.
He wants to make us spirited.
He helps to cross the barrier of hell,
but we just enjoy.
A good inventor wastes a part of life
for to create a mysterious technique,
but we just enjoy.
A physician saves a life, and
tries to make an embodiment.
We get a change (a new life),
but we just enjoy.
A sophisticated well doer of society
dedicates his thoughts of integrity.
We only leave him a comment for recommendation as a
price,
and we just enjoy.
So, all those are no doubt great.,
but we just enjoy . . . .
We should indulge ourselves to employ (to assist them).

Your Last Smile

I saw and noticed your last smile.
It was fantastic but mystic a little bit.
Now, I can complete my hemistich.
I got the newness!
You left a note—
This might revert me and my earlier past.
So, I revere your love,
And I reveal it perfectly.

You know, I was being scoured for an unknown desire
(for some time).
I was going to stiffen my heart.
But you, at the same time, came and showed me the
exact path.
You saved me, otherwise
I would be strayed.
Now, I've made my contrivance stronger.
I can originate my feelings more perfectly (than earlier).
Though I've lost something,
But I got you once—
And your last smile.

Yours . . . .

The propaganda, which I've achieved, is yours.

The theory of life, that I've got, is solely yours.

This piteous life once had become worthless,

But, lastly I conquered.

Now, it placates me—and I think,

It should be claimed as your kindness and your immensurable dedication.

I know, you are beautiful but a plain-looking.

I am just a plain-spoken fellow.

If our hearts would meet with each other,

It would be a moment of unspeakable joy, full of sweetness, and it would be mellow.

My every word always implicates you, and you know it.

I will always bear this probity.

I never live in insincerity.

That's why, I always put it down in every single line of my verse, and I still try to use too many words (only for you).

Yes, this life is fully indebted to you.

It's yours.

Yes, yours . . . .